She Stood There
a poem by
"Twinkle" Marie Manning

Copyright © Marie Manning
Poem: "She Stood There" 1989, Book: December 2016

All Rights Reserved
including the right of reproduction of this book,
copying, or storage in any form or means, including
electronic, without prior written permission of the author.
*Should you wish to print the poem to use in a spiritual or religious
service or private or public event, you have the poet's permission
to do so from this page: www.TwinklesPlace.org/SheStoodThere
Please always credit her for her work. And please consider
contributing to sustaining such works:
www.MatrikaPress.com/sustainingpoetry*

ISBN 978-1-946088-33-8
Library of Congress Control Number: 2016919951

1. Poetry 2. Choices 3. Spirituality 4. Life Changes
5. Unitarian Universalism 6. Title

Matrika Press
164 Lancey Street
Pittsfield, Maine 04967
(760) 889-5428

First Edition

Printed in the USA

Poet's images by Orion Menchaca

Beach Cover images by "Twinkle" Marie Manning

Poet's Dedication

To My Daughter,
Morgan Bailey,

May the paths to
your heartsongs
always be revealed.

I love you.

She Stood There

In the midst of the shadows

In a darkness that haunted

She stood there

still,

silent,

sorry,

sad.

Plenty of time to think of
 days gone by

Loves lost,

loves gained;

her sorrow remembered

She stood there

still,

silent,

sorry.

The seconds ticked to minutes

The minutes onto hours

She stood there

still,

silent.

She realized

she could not have it all

So she settled for less;

but yet only the best

She stood there

still.

With her eyes wide open,

her head held high

With a decision in mind

She stood there no more.

She Stood There
by "Twinkle" Marie Manning

In the midst of the shadows
In a darkness that haunted
She stood there still, silent, sorry, sad.

Plenty of time to think of days gone by
Loves lost, loves gained; her sorrow remembered
She stood there still, silent, sorry.

The seconds ticked to minutes
The minutes onto hours
She stood there still, silent.

She realized she could not have it all
So she settled for less; but yet only the best
She stood there still.

With her eyes wide open, her head held high
With a decision in mind
She stood there no more.

Originally penned in 1989,
Prince Edward Island, Canada.
First published in 2009
"Poetry to Feed the Spirit"
Poets of Central Florida anthology.
Included in Matrika Press Women of Spirit anthology 2014/2016.

"Twinkle" Marie Manning's poetry has been included in spiritual rituals, funerals, memorials, wedding ceremonies, blessingways, and coming-of-age gatherings in many locations around the world. She is a member of the Unitarian Universalist Society for Community Ministries and the founder of UU Talks and Matrika Press.

Matrika Press is an independent publishing house dedicated to publishing works in alignment with Unitarian Universalist values and principles.
Its fiscal sponsor is UU Women and Religion.
(www.uuwr.org)
Matrika derives its name from the 50 letters of the Sanskrit alphabet called "the mothers" aka "Matrika." Kali Ma used the letters to form words, and from the words formed all things...as with the Bible: *"in the beginning was the Word."*
People of all backgrounds and faiths agree:
Words are powerful.
More than that: *Their vibrations are creative forces;
they bring all things into being.*
Matrika Press publishes anthologies, memoirs, poetry, prayer and ritual manuscripts, and other books to bring transformation to the world. We *do* accept unsolicited manuscripts at this time. Should you wish to Publish your work, visit our website.

www.MatrikaPress.com

AVAILABLE NOW FROM MATRIKA PRESS

This book is a compilation of women sojourners, sages, mystics, witches, shaman, medicine women, ministers, philosophers, therapists, life coaches, yogis, and more. Their journeys. Their stories. Their teachings and practices. Essays, Poetry, Art, Rituals and Prayers. This anthology is full of useful tools and powerful messages for everyone who is on a spiritual journey to embrace and enjoy. Beloved Contributors include:

- *Anna Huckabee Tull • Bernadette Rombough • Deb Elbaum*
- *Deborah Diamond • Debra Wilson Guttas • Grace Ventura*
- *Janeen Barnett • JoAnne Bassett • Judy Ann Foster*
- *Julie Matheson • Kate Early • Kate Kavanagh • Katherine Glass*
- *Kris Oster • Lea M. Hill • Meghan Gilroy • Morwen Two Feathers*
- *Rustie MacDonald • Shamanaca • Sharon Hinckley • Shawna Allard*
- *Shiloh Sophia • Susan Feathers • Tiffany Cano • Tory Londergan*
- *"Twinkle" Marie Manning • Tziporah Kingsbury • Valerie Sorrentino*

www.MatrikaPress.com

Seventh Principle Studies & First Source Explorations

The Seventh UU Principle is: *"Respect for the interdependent web of all existence of which we are a part."*

The First Source UUs draw faith from is: *"Direct experience of that transcending mystery and wonder, affirmed in all cultures, which moves us to a renewal of the spirit and an openness to the forces which create and uphold life."*

Evidence to support such is found within the pages of ***The Way of Power***.

www.MatrikaPress.com

Fourth Source Explorations

Two of our focuses at Matrika Press are to preserve texts and thoughts of our ancestors, and to create publications that share the values and principles of Unitarian Universalism. This allegorical story by David Starr Jordan is a tale about the search for spiritual meaning. Symbolic of Jesus Christ's ministry, it succinctly embodies our Christian heritage and the fourth of the six sources we draw our faith from, namely that which calls us to respond to God's love by loving our neighbors as ourselves.

www.MatrikaPress.com

RECOMMENDED SELECTIONS FROM SKINNER HOUSE

Reaching for the Sun
Rev. Angela Herrera's book of meditations, prayers and invocations provide inspiration to readers and serve as a resource to those seeking powerful liturgical words, grounded in the experiences of everyday life.

Evening Tide
This book of mediations by Elizabeth Tarbox helps readers to face the darker moments of life, the challenging circumstances that call us to live more fully even when we feel our most empty.

Stirring the Nation's Heart: Eighteen Stories of Prophetic Unitarians and Universalists of the 19th Century by Polly Peterson
Eighteen compelling stories from the lives of some of the nineteenth-century Transcendentalists and reformers who played key roles in Unitarian Universalist history.

http://www.uua.org/publications/skinnerhouse

RECOMMENDED SELECTIONS FROM BEACON PRESS

Claiming the Spirit Within
This wonderful book, edited by Rev. Marilyn Sewell, is a beautiful sourcebook of poetry and prose. A rich and diverse anthology dedicated to the praise of life, it presents the sacredness that emerges when women immerse fully in living lives of spirit while embracing the physical. More than 300 poems celebrating all aspects of women's lives.

http://www.beacon.org/

www.ingramcontent.com/pod-product-compliance
Lightning Source LLC
Chambersburg PA
CBHW071548080526
44588CB00011B/1834